RUBY and the DRAGON !!

Gareth Owen

Illustrated by
Bob Wilson

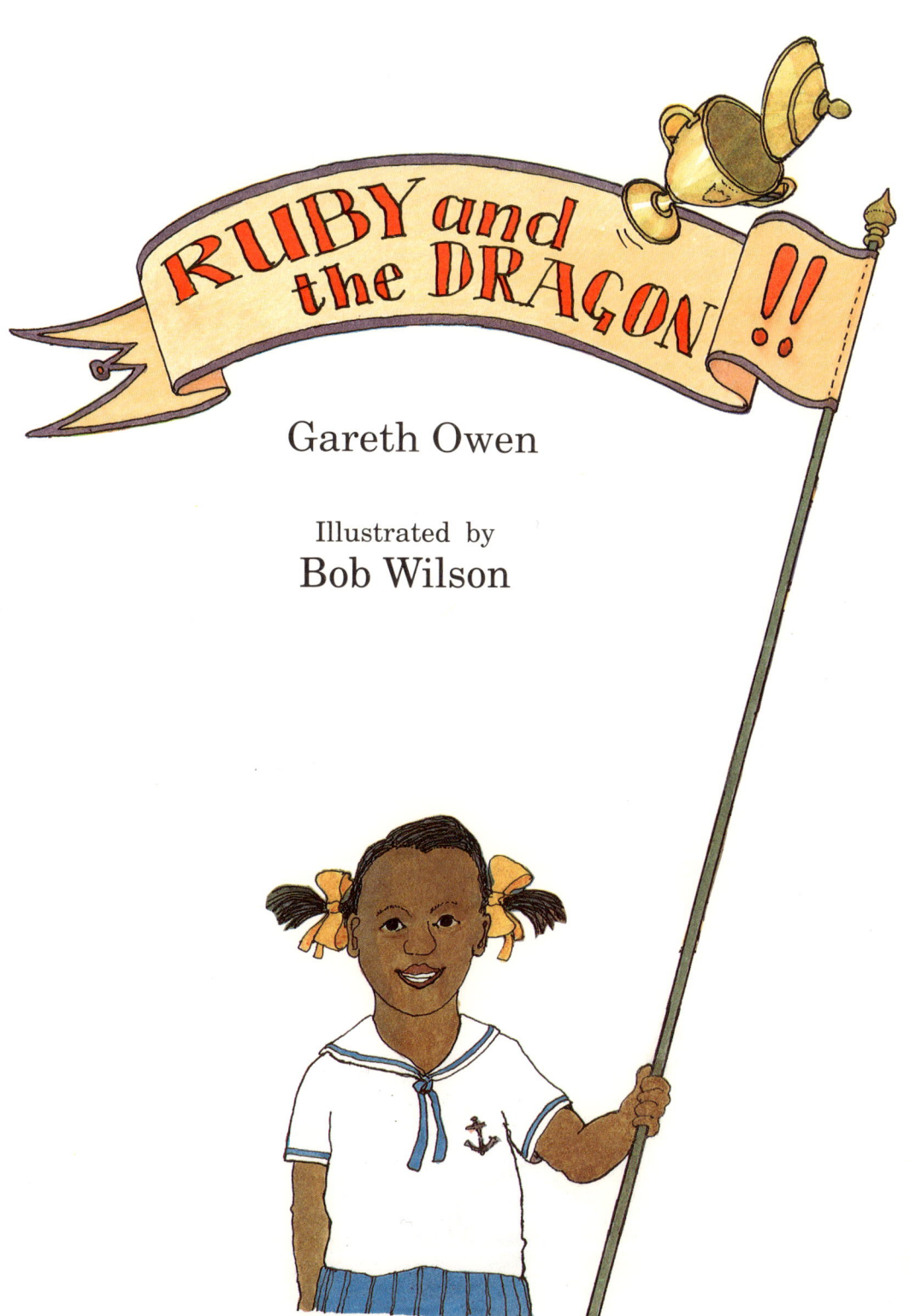

COLLINS

Class 4 was in school.

Miss Williams said,

We're going to do something special today.

She brought out a big box.

Everyone wondered what was in the box.

Is it a doll?

Is it a football?

Is it a pork-pie?

Is everybody here?

Please, Miss.

Ruby was late.

We can't open the box until Ruby is here.

Ruby was always late for school.

She saw the poster on the wall.

Ruby liked animals.

I'd like to be a parrot or a polar bear, or best of all I'd like to be a....

The crossing lady said,

Shouldn't you be in school?

ARRRGH! I'm a crocodile,

replied Ruby.

Ruby walked into the playground.

Ruby tried on the dress.

What do you think?

Very nice, Ruby.

Angela, you try the dress on.

Angela tried on the dress.

It fitted her perfectly.

I am princess Angela.

I never really wanted to be princess, anyway.

You have to be soppy to be princess.

That will do, Ruby.

Ruby tried on the helmet.

Next we have - the dragon. Prince Raymond kills the dragon. The dragon costume fits over your head; nobody will see you.

Who would like to play the dragon?

The dragon has a loud voice. Is there anyone in the class with a loud voice?

Miss Williams said,

Ruby. You will play the dragon.

Ruby didn't want to be the dragon.

Ruby wore her costume every day.

She wore it at mealtimes.

She wore it in the street.

The postman was surprised.

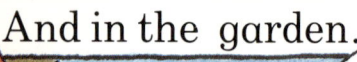

And in the garden.

The cat was surprised.

She wore it in bed.

At school they practised every day.

The day of the play came round.   Everybody was in the hall.

The headmaster was there.   The Mayor was there.

Ruby's mummy and daddy were there.

Ruby was nervous.   Angela was nervous.   Raymond was nervous.

In the dressing room Ruby practised her lines.

Miss Williams looked in.

Miss Williams made a speech.

Everybody clapped.

The school was empty; everybody was at the play.

The money was on the headmaster's desk.

The cups were on the shelf.

Mr Jones was asleep.

Two men climbed in through the window.

They were burglars.

We'll steal the money and the cups.

The school was empty.

They peeped through the door.

The two men crept towards the headmaster's office.

Mr Jones did not wake up.

said Miss Williams.

said Ruby.

She heard her line.

She practised swinging her head like a dragon.

She knocked down a tin of powder paint.
The powder went up her nose.

She found the right door.

Ruby was not very good at directions,

or at remembering things.

She went down the wrong corridor.

She turned left.

On the stage Angela said,

Prince Raymond, listen I think I can hear the dragon coming this way.

But she was wrong.

The dragon was lost.

Mr Jones was asleep. The two burglars were hard at work.

Everybody was waiting for Ruby.

Miss Williams went to the dressing room.

Ruby wasn't in the cupboard.

Ruby was outside the staff-room door.

She took a deep breath, and burst through the door.

It was the wrong door.

Everybody was still waiting for Ruby.

Miss Williams was following the dragon's footprints.

Ruby was outside the headmaster's door.

She took a big breath...

The burglars ran off down the corridor.   Ruby ran after them.

Mr Jones went into the headmaster's office.

Miss Williams arrived.

Miss Williams ran off down the corridor.

Mr Jones rang the police.

Everybody was *still* waiting for the dragon.

Then, at last,
they heard footsteps.
They were coming towards
the stage.
And so, in a very loud voice,
Angela cried out...

and Miss Williams ran onto the stage.

Then two men ran onto the stage....

followed by a policeman...   and a caretaker...

and a dragon.

Ruby chased Raymond around the stage.

The audience cheered. Ruby was the winner.

The curtains closed.

It was the end of the play.

But it was not the end of the story.

But the Mayor was making a speech.

Miss Williams stepped forward.

The Mayor gave her some flowers.

Everybody cheered...

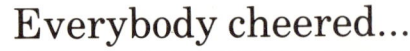

...and cheered.

Miss Williams smiled. The Mayor smiled. The Headmaster smiled.

The policeman said,

Ruby had gone.

Ruby was waiting for the bus.   She'd had enough of play-acting.

The bus conductor said,   said Ruby.

The bus took her home.

THE END.

William Collins Sons & Co. Ltd.
London · Glasgow · Sydney · Auckland
Toronto · Johannesburg

First published 1990

© text Gareth Owen 1990
© illustrations Bob Wilson 1990

A CIP catalogue record for this book is available from the British Library

ISBN 0 00 195406 7

Printed and bound in Portugal